Born in the Wild: Baby Animals

Rick Raymos

rourkeeducationalmedia.com

Scan for Related Titles
and Teacher Resources

Teaching Focus:

Concepts of Print: One to One Correspondence- Point to each word as you read.

Before Reading:

Building Academic Vocabulary and Background Knowledge

Before reading a book, it is important to set the stage for your child or students by using pre-reading strategies. This will help them develop their vocabulary, increase their reading comprehension, and make connections across the curriculum.

1. *Read the title and look at the cover. Let's make predictions about what this book will be about.*
2. *Take a picture walk by talking about the pictures/photographs in the book. Implant the vocabulary as you take the picture walk. Be sure to talk about the text features such as headings, Table of Contents, glossary, bolded words, captions, charts/ diagrams, or Index.*
3. *Have students read the first page of text with you then have students read the remaining text.*
4. *Strategy Talk – use to assist students while reading.*
    - *Get your mouth ready*
    - *Look at the picture*
    - *Think…does it make sense*
    - *Think…does it look right*
    - *Think…does it sound right*
    - *Chunk it – by looking for a part you know*
5. *Read it again.*
6. *After reading the book complete the activities below.*

Content Area Vocabulary

Use glossary words in a sentence.

herd
intruder
jaws
joey
predator
protect

After Reading:

Comprehension and Extension Activity

After reading the book, work on the following questions with your child or students in order to check their level of reading comprehension and content mastery.

1. *How does an elephant help its calf stay with the herd? (Summarize)*
2. *What are the mothers protecting their babies from? (Summarize)*
3. *How do animal parents prepare their babies to live on their own? (Asking questions)*
4. *How do the adults in your life protect you? (Text to self connection)*

Extension Activity

Choose one of the animals from the book. Write a short story where the parents protect the baby. Make sure you include facts and a drawing that matches your story.

Every family has a special bond,
both at home and beyond.

Animal Families

In the animal world, parents look after their babies. They want to make sure the babies are strong and ready to survive in the wild.

Zebras

Squirrels

Animal parents keep their babies safe. They teach them to find food. With strong babies, the species is able to survive.

Harp Seal

A harp seal pup plays on the Arctic ice. Then, CR-A-CK! A **predator** breaks through the ice. The mother harp seal sniffs the air to find her pup.

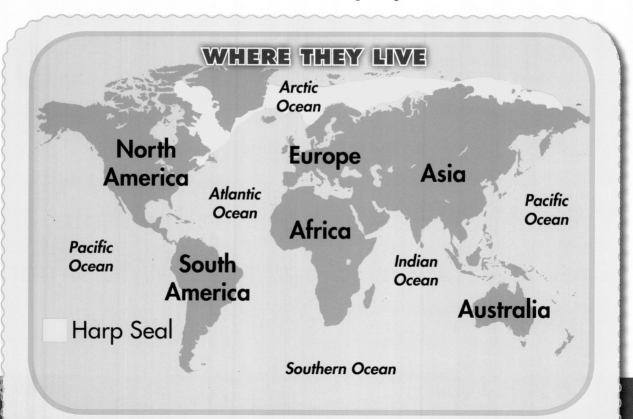

WHERE THEY LIVE

Arctic Ocean

North America

Europe

Asia

Atlantic Ocean

Pacific Ocean

Africa

Pacific Ocean

South America

Indian Ocean

Australia

Harp Seal

Southern Ocean

Harp seal mothers know their babies by their smell. The mothers keep their babies safe.

Harp seals spend most of their time on the ice or in the water. They can stay underwater for up to 15 minutes.

Harp Seals

Asian Elephant

Not that way! The mother elephant grips the calf's tail to show him the way. The babies stay with the **herd**.

Male elephants leave their mothers when they are 13 years old. Females stay with their mothers their whole lives. The mothers keep their babies safe.

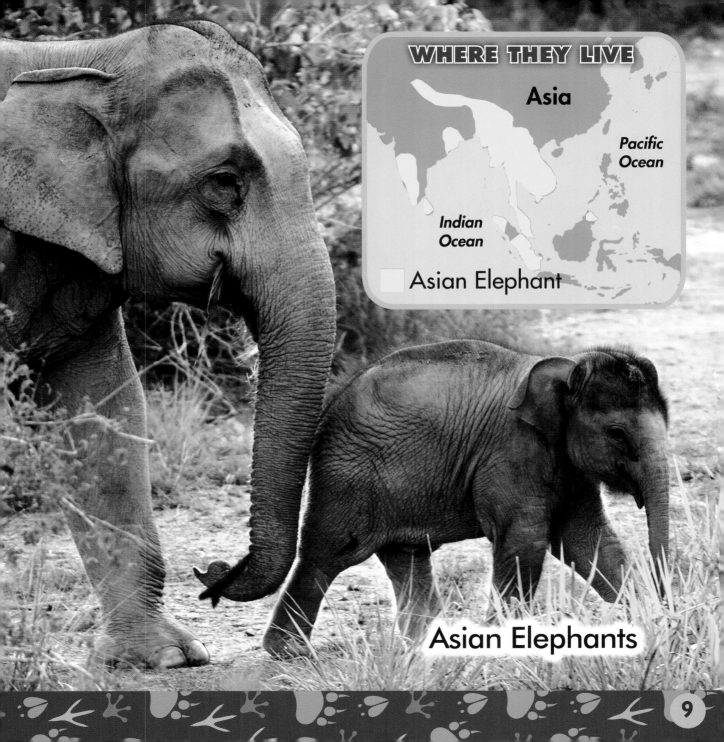

WHERE THEY LIVE

Asia

Pacific
Ocean

Indian
Ocean

Asian Elephant

Asian Elephants

Black Bear

A bobcat wanders into the black bear's home. The mother bear sends her cubs to hide. She roars and swipes at the **intruder**, ready to attack.

Black Bears

WHERE THEY LIVE

Arctic Ocean

North America

Europe

Asia

Atlantic Ocean

Pacific Ocean

Africa

Pacific Ocean

South America

Indian Ocean

Australia

Black Bear

Black bear mothers stay with their babies for about two years. The mothers **protect** their young.

Cheetah

Snatch! The mother cheetah catches a baby gazelle and brings it back to her cubs. They practice taking down the animal.

Cheetahs

Cheetah mothers teach their young to hunt when they are 6 months old. The mothers keep their babies fed.

WHERE THEY LIVE

Asia

Africa

Atlantic Ocean

Indian Ocean

Cheetah

Nile Crocodile

Knock, knock. The baby crocodile is ready to come out of its shell. The mother helps her baby from the egg.

WHERE THEY LIVE

Africa

Atlantic Ocean

Nile Crocodile

Nile Crocodile

Nile crocodile mothers carry their babies in their toothy **jaws**. The mothers keep their babies safe.

Eastern Gray Kangaroo

Peek-a-boo! The joey's head pops out of its mother's pouch. Inside the pouch, the **joey** stays warm and gets plenty of milk to drink.

Baby kangaroos stay in their mothers' pouch for two months after they are born. The mothers keep their babies safe.

Eastern Gray Kangaroos

WHERE THEY LIVE

Indian Ocean

Australia

Eastern Gray Kangaroo

17

Mallard Duck

The little ducklings follow the lead of their mother. They swim and waddle after her while she looks for food.

WHERE THEY LIVE

Arctic Ocean

North America

Europe

Asia

Atlantic Ocean

Pacific Ocean

Pacific Ocean

Africa

South America

Australia

Mallard Duck

Mallard duck mothers show their babies how and where to find food. The mothers teach their babies.

Mallard ducks eat by tipping forward in the water and eating underwater plants.

Mallard Ducks

Green Sea Turtle

At night, the green sea turtle mother crawls onto the beach. She quietly digs a hole in the sand and buries her eggs.

WHERE THEY LIVE

Arctic Ocean

North America

Atlantic Ocean

Europe

Asia

Pacific Ocean

Africa

Pacific Ocean

Indian Ocean

South America

Australia

Southern Ocean

Green Sea Turtle

Green sea turtle mothers lay their eggs on the same beach where they were born. The mothers keep their eggs safe.

When animal parents look after their young, the species is better able to survive.

Green Sea Turtle

Photo Glossary

herd (HURD): A big group of animals that lives together.

intruder (in-TROOD-ur): An unwanted guest.

jaws (JAWS): The bones that hold an animal's teeth in place.

 **joey** (JOH-ee): A baby kangaroo.

 **predator** (PRED-uh-tur): An animal that hunts other animals as food.

 **protect** (pruh-TEKT): To keep safe from danger.

Index

About the Author

Rick Raymos is a writer and nature-lover. He loves to visit zoos and see unique animals from all around the world. Rick lives in New York City with his dog Reed.

Meet The Author!
www.meetREMauthors.com

Websites

animals.nationalgeographic.com/animals/photos/baby-animals
www.enchantedlearning.com/subjects/animals/Animalbabies.shtml
www.animalplanet.com/mammals/kangaroo-quiz.htm

www.rourkeeducationalmedia.com

PHOTO CREDITS: Cover, page 14: ©Trevor kelly; title page: ©Volodymyr Goinyk; page 3: ©Christopher Futcher; page 4: ©Mattia D'Antonio; page 5: ©Kelly Nelson; page 7: © Vladimir Melnik; page 9: ©Thanakon Khongman; page 10: ©Dennis Donohue; page 11, 23 (bottom): ©Scenic Shutterbug; page 12: ©George Lamson; page 12: ©nicolamargaret; page 15, 22 (bottom): ©wcpmedia; page 17, 23 (top): ©kjuuurs; page 18-19: ©Alex Baker; page 21: ©German; page 22 : ©Vladyslav Morozov (top), ©Micha Kloutwijk (middle); page 23: ©Grafissimo (middle)

Edited by: Jill Sherman
Cover design by: Jen Thomas
Interior design by: Rhea Magaro

Library of Congress PCN Data

Born in the Wild: Baby Animals / Rick Raymos
(Close Up on Amazing Animals)
ISBN (hard cover)(alk. paper) 978-1-62717-637-8
ISBN (soft cover) 978-1-62717-759-7
ISBN (e-Book) 978-1-62717-880-8
Library of Congress Control Number: 2014934205

Printed in the United States of America, North Mankato, Minnesota

Also Available as:

ROURKE'S
e-Books